SCIENCE WORLD

LIVING THINGS

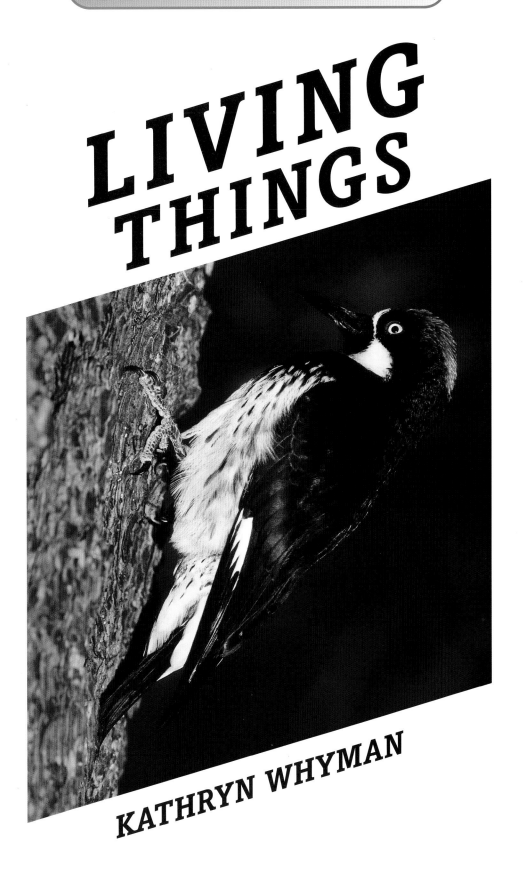

KATHRYN WHYMAN

Franklin Watts
London • Sydney

© Archon Press 2003

Produced by
Archon Press Ltd
28 Percy Street
London W1T 2BZ

New edition first published in
Great Britain in 2003 by
Franklin Watts
96 Leonard Street
London EC2A 4XD

Original edition published as
Simply Science – Living Things

ISBN 0–7496–5391–4

Editor:
Katie Harker

Designer:
Pete Bennett – PBD

Picture Researcher:
Brian Hunter Smart

Illustrator:
Louise Nevett

Printed in UAE

CONTENTS

INTRODUCTION

Our world is home to many millions of living things. From the hot, dry deserts to the frozen polar regions, at the depths of the oceans, and even inside the bodies of other creatures! All living things are specially adapted to enable them to survive in their different environments.

Living things may look very different, but they all share some basic characteristics: they need oxygen and 'nutrients' for nourishment; they move and grow; they get rid of waste substances; they react to things around them; and they can also reproduce.

Polar bears are specially adapted to live in the cold extremes of the polar regions.

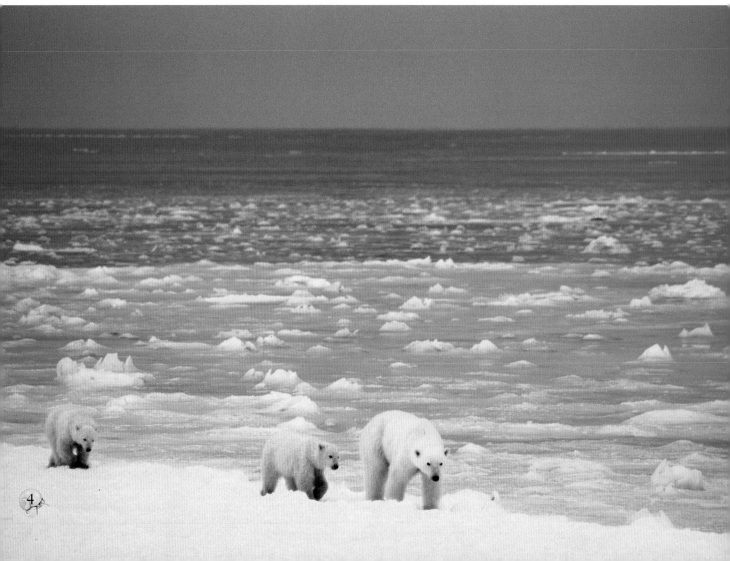

In this book you will find out how living things cope with the changes which are constantly taking place around them. You will learn how living things have grown and evolved over millions of years. You will also discover that some living things communicate, and that all living things depend on each other for their survival.

Right: Chameleons change the colour and pattern of their skin, to blend in with their surroundings and protect themselves from attack.

Lions are camouflaged in the hot, dry plains of Africa, where they hunt for unsuspecting prey.

IS IT ALIVE?

Imagine you were looking at a waxwork model of a child. The model might confuse you at first. It may look very realistic and even share many of the physical features of a child. But you would soon be able to tell that the waxwork was not a living thing.

A real child can move. A child needs to eat and breathe to survive, and gets rid of waste materials, like faeces and urine, from its body. A child can see and hear things happening nearby and will act accordingly. Eventually the child will grow and may even have children of its own. The waxwork model may appear to be very lifelike but it can do none of these things.

 Living things can move from place to place, sometimes very quickly, like these human sprinters.

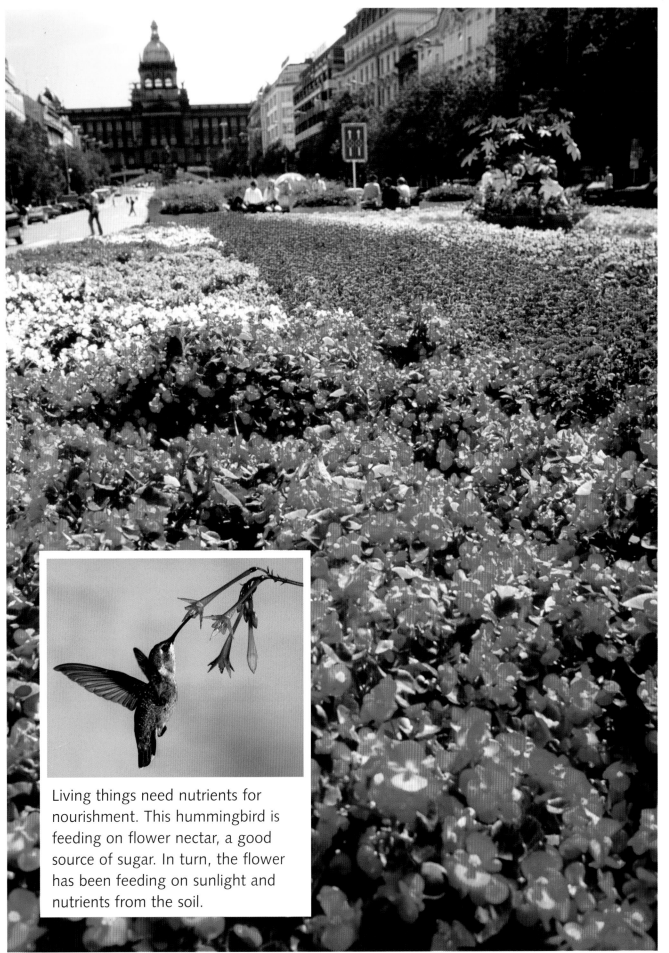

Living things need nutrients for nourishment. This hummingbird is feeding on flower nectar, a good source of sugar. In turn, the flower has been feeding on sunlight and nutrients from the soil.

We plant many kinds of trees, shrubs and flowers in public places and in our gardens.

THE VARIETY OF LIFE

There are about two million different types of living things today! Although they share similar features, there are also great differences between them. People have found it useful to sort living things into groups. The two largest groups are the plant and the animal kingdoms.

Within these groups there are many different types, or 'species'. So scientists divide the plant and animal kingdoms into smaller groups. Animals are firstly divided into those which have backbones, the 'vertebrates', and those which do not, the 'invertebrates'. Plants have also been divided into many different groups, that distinguish between their structure and their leaf or flowering cycles.

The animal kingdom

Most animals are invertebrates (without a backbone). For example, earthworms, butterflies, spiders and crabs are just a few invertebrates. Vertebrates can be put into five groups: fish, amphibians (vertebrates which spend part of their lives in water and part on land), birds, reptiles and mammals. Mammals are the only animals which produce milk to feed their young.

REPTILES

MAMMALS

INVERTEBRATES

FISH

AMPHIBIANS

BIRDS

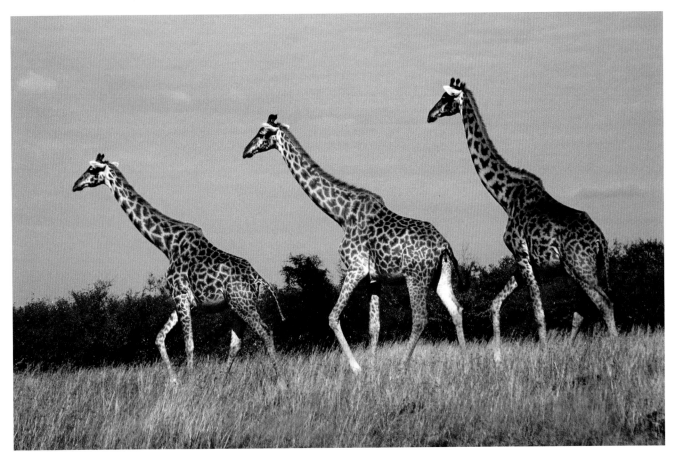

Giraffes are found in the open woodlands and grasslands of Africa. They are the tallest living animal.

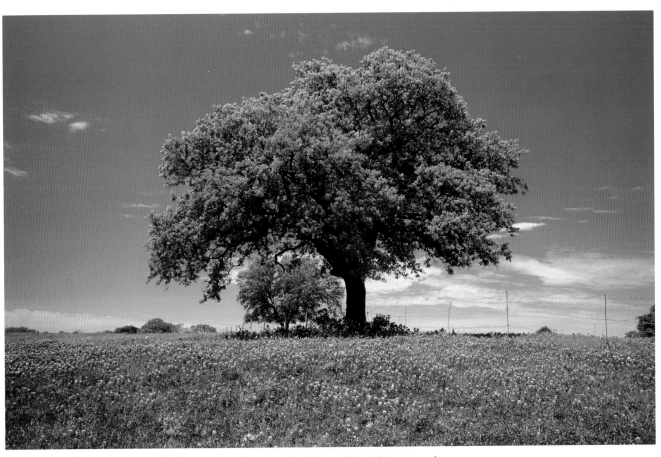

Many different types of plant species can be found in this meadow.

EVOLUTION

Where did all the different types of living things come from? Nobody knows for certain, but many scientists think that plants and animals have gradually developed, or 'evolved', over millions of years. As they have changed, they have become better adapted to survive.

For example, millions of years ago plants had no flowers. They relied solely on the wind and the rain to transport their pollen to other plants, so that new seeds could develop. But over time, plants developed simple flowers to attract insects. Insects accidently pick up sticky pollen as they feed on flower nectar, and carry it to nearby plants, helping the flowers to reproduce.

Human beings may have evolved from ape-like animals. These developed the ability to stand upright on just two feet, so that they could then use their hands for other things. Over millions of years they learnt how to use tools and developed these to become successful hunters.

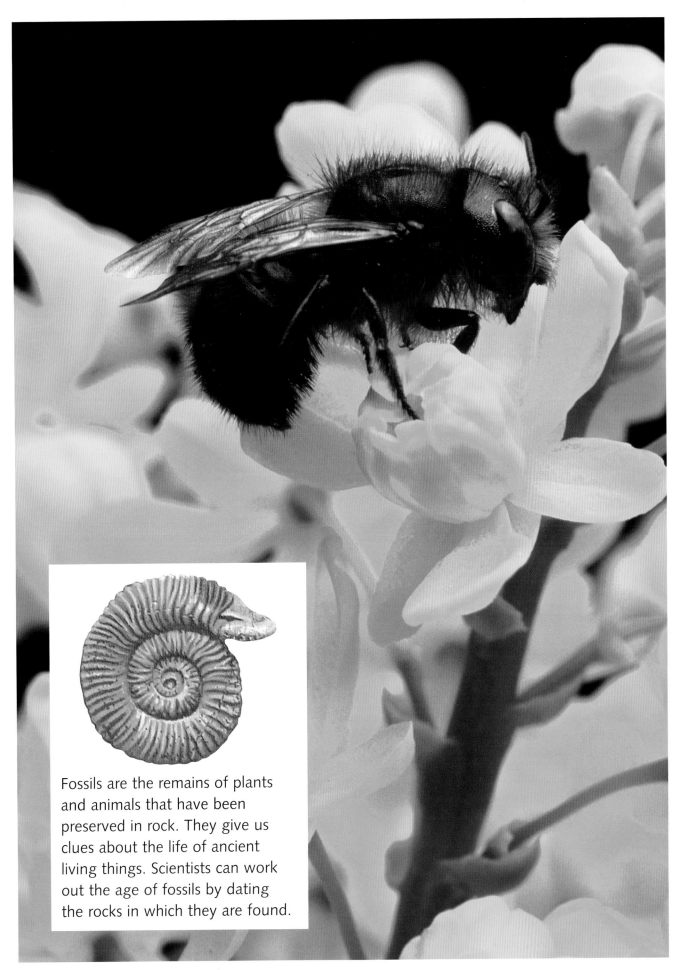

Fossils are the remains of plants and animals that have been preserved in rock. They give us clues about the life of ancient living things. Scientists can work out the age of fossils by dating the rocks in which they are found.

Insect-pollinated plants tend to have fragrant, brightly coloured flowers to attract insects.

CELLS

All living things are made up of tiny building blocks called 'cells'. Cells are too small to see without a microscope. Some living things have one cell, but the human body consists of about a hundred trillion cells!

Almost all cells contain a nucleus. The nucleus is very important as it controls everything that happens inside the cell. Around the nucleus is a jelly-like substance called 'cytoplasm'. Here, lots of chemicals are stored. Around the cytoplasm is a very thin 'skin' called the cell membrane. This holds the contents of the cell together and controls what enters and leaves the cell. Plants and animals have different types of cells. These cells are all designed for a particular job.

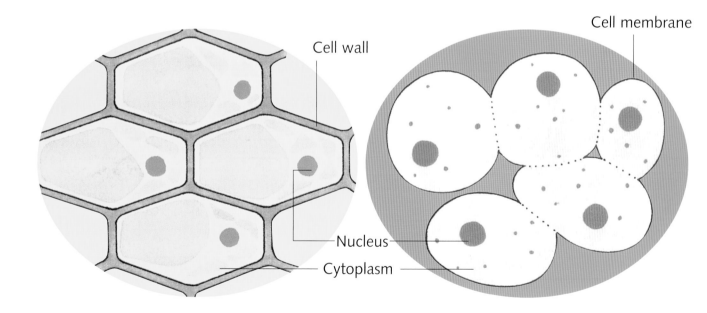

Cell wall

Cell membrane

Nucleus

Cytoplasm

Plant cells

Plant cells are each surrounded by a 'cell wall' made of cellulose, which gives the plant structure and support. They each have a nucleus and cytoplasm. Plant cells usually have a very regular shape.

Animal cells

Animal cells don't have any cell walls (just a cell membrane). This is because animals use other ways of supporting themselves, such as skeletons. Animal cells are usually irregular in shape.

Special cells have caused pigmentation in these zebras' coats, creating a striped camouflage.

A leaf under a microscope clearly shows the structure of a plant cell.

FEEDING AND BREATHING

Living things need certain substances to move, grow and keep themselves alive. Animals eat plants or other animals as their main source of nutrition.

This food is chemically complicated and must be reduced to simpler materials by a process called 'digestion'. Chemicals in the body break down the nutrients in food, which the body then uses for growth and energy. Waste materials are then excreted by the body.

Sun's energy

Carbon dioxide

Oxygen

Food

Water & minerals

Photosynthesis

Plants and animals depend on each other for feeding and breathing. Plants take carbon dioxide from the air and absorb water and minerals from the soil. They use the Sun's energy to convert these simple substances into sugars and starches and produce oxygen. This is called 'photosynthesis'.

Animals, like gorillas, use plants as a source of food. They also breathe in the oxygen that plants release. Animals produce carbon dioxide which they breathe out and they excrete waste water and chemicals from their bodies. Plants depend on all these substances.

Plants need oxygen in order to carry out certain life processes. Plants use photosynthesis to produce oxygen but they also absorb oxygen from the soil (through their roots) and from the air (through small holes in their leaves).

At night, plants take oxygen from the air because there is not enough sunlight for photosynthesis to take place. During the day plants produce their own oxygen – much more than they need. This excess oxygen is released into the air.

Plants provide oxygen for humans and animals to breathe.

Squirrels need to eat about half a kilogram of food a week to maintain an active life.

GETTING FROM PLACE TO PLACE

Most animals have to move to find their food and to avoid predators and other dangers. Many of these animals have muscles to help them move. Muscles help fish to swim, birds and insects to fly and many animals to walk and run.

Plants move by growing in different directions. When water is in short supply, plant roots grow deeper into the soil to find it. Shoots grow taller to find more sunlight. Plants also need to move their pollen and seeds. Pollen and seeds are 'dispersed' – spread around – from their parent plant so that they have their own space to grow. They may be carried by animals, water or the wind.

Most snakes get from place to place by throwing their bodies into curves. When a snake moves, waves of muscular contraction flow from head to tail. Its sides also push against irregularities on the ground (represented by the orange arrows in the diagram).

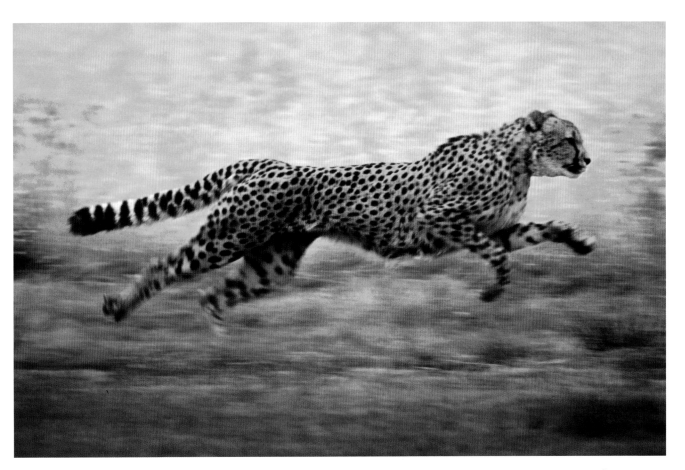

Virtually every part of a cheetah's body has been adapted to maximise its running speed.

Climbing plants, like ivy, use walls and other structures for support, and grow towards the sunlight.

A CHANGING ENVIRONMENT

In order to survive, living things must be able to detect changes in their environment and react to them. This includes adapting to changing weather conditions and the threat of living things that may approach them.

Animals have up to five senses – sight, smell, hearing, taste and touch – to help them to detect changes around them. A dog may react to the smell of food by running towards it; an earthworm will react to light by burrowing underground; and a chameleon changes its skin colour and patterns to match its background. Plants don't have senses of this kind but they can still detect changes in their environment.

This sea anemone reacts to touch...

... by retracting its tentacles.

Plants can react to certain changes in their environment. We have seen how plants grow towards light and water. This sunflower gradually turns as it follows the path of the Sun during the day. Some flowers, such as lilies, open during the day and close at night. Plants are remarkably sensitive to heat, light, drought, certain chemicals and gravity, but they have no special organs for detecting change.

Arctic foxes stay camouflaged all year round because their fur turns from brown to white in winter.

REACTING TO CHANGE

When we react to a changing environment, conditions *inside* our bodies change. Your body's main instinct is survival, so it reacts to potentially dangerous situations.

When you exercise, most of the energy in your body is released as heat energy, and your temperature rises. To lower your body temperature, blood moves to the surface of your skin where it can cool down. Water also evaporates from your skin as sweat, helping to cool your body. During the winter months, physical changes can also help an animal to hibernate, whilst food is scarce.

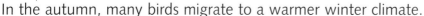

In the winter months, some animals, like dormice and bats, are no longer able to find food. Changes take place inside their bodies to help them survive this situation, and they 'hibernate'. The animal curls up into a ball and 'sleeps' for the winter. Its body gradually gets colder, its heartbeat slows down and it breathes less often. In this condition animals use little energy. They can survive without eating and live off stores of fat inside their body.

In the autumn, many birds migrate to a warmer winter climate.

It is important to drink after excercise to replace lost fluids.

GROWTH AND REPRODUCTION

As plants and animals develop, they grow and get larger and heavier. How does this growth take place? We know that living things take substances, like food, into their bodies. Some of these substances become part of body cells. Cells get bigger until they cannot grow any more and they divide into two. As more cells are formed, a living thing grows.

When living things are fully developed they are able to 'reproduce' and create new members of their species. Most living things in the animal world reproduce when special 'sex cells' from the mother and father join together. As this cell grows and divides, a new living thing develops.

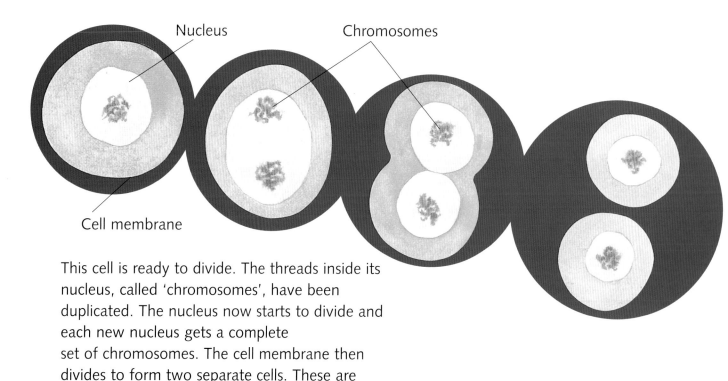

Nucleus   Chromosomes

Cell membrane

This cell is ready to divide. The threads inside its nucleus, called 'chromosomes', have been duplicated. The nucleus now starts to divide and each new nucleus gets a complete set of chromosomes. The cell membrane then divides to form two separate cells. These are identical to the original cell with the same number of chromosomes. They will grow and eventually divide themselves into two new cells.

This calf will grow and develop for up to seven years before it becomes fully-grown.

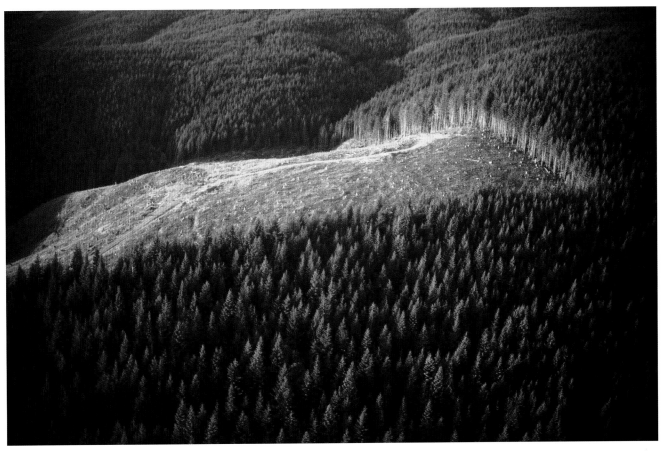

Trees grow at different rates. Yew trees grow for 1,000 years, whilst pine trees mature in 30 years.

COMMUNICATING

Many living things can pass information to each other – they 'communicate'. The expression on the face of a cat may show that it is angry or frightened. Bees perform complicated dances to tell each other where to find good sources of food, and monkeys show each other affection by grooming each other and cuddling their young.

Some animals communicate by producing chemicals. Cheetahs mark out their territories by spraying urine and scent onto plants. Birds and mammals also communicate by making sounds. Humans, as the most intelligent of all animals, have developed the most complicated and successful form of communication – speech.

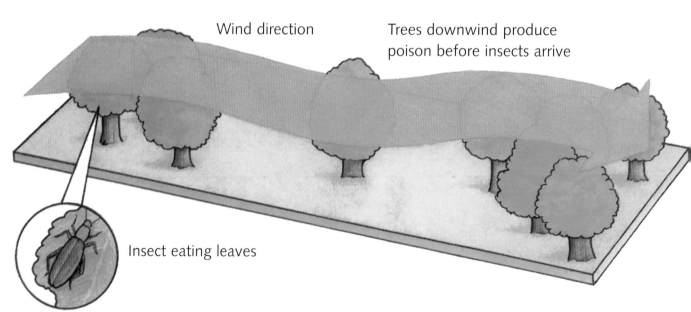

Wind direction

Trees downwind produce poison before insects arrive

Insect eating leaves

We usually associate communication with animals, but some plants are also able to communicate. For example, a few trees produce poison in their leaves when they are attacked by insects. Some of these trees can actually send warning signals to nearby trees. A chemical signal is passed through the air, enabling trees downwind to prepare for the attack. In a similar way, plants also communicate with insects. If corn, cotton or tobacco plants are attacked by caterpillars they emit chemicals that simultaneously attract parasitic wasps. These wasps eat the caterpillars and discourage other worms and moths from laying their eggs on the plants.

Monkeys use a number of vocal, visual and tactile forms of communication.

Dolphins communicate using a system of whistles, squeaks, moans, trills and clicks.

Elephants show aggression by locking tusks and wrestling with their trunks.

LIVING WITH EACH OTHER

A living thing cannot live alone. It depends on other living things to supply the materials it needs to survive. We have seen how animals rely on plants for their food. Animals which only eat plants are called 'herbivores'. Animals which eat other animals are called 'carnivores'. A series of living things which feed on each other make up a 'food chain'. If one of the members of the chain is removed all the others may be affected.

Often, several food chains interlink as many animals feed on a variety of plants or animals. The chains together make a 'food web'.

A food chain
The insects in this food chain feed on the leaves of plants. Some of these insects are eaten by frogs. Frogs, in turn, are eaten by snakes. Hawks are the final carnivores in this chain. When the hawks and other members of the chain die, their bodies decay and are returned to the soil. The nutrients in the soil help new plants to grow.

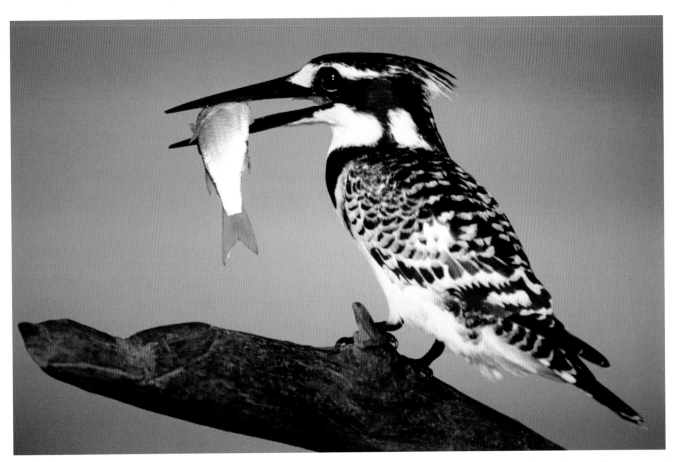

Kingfishers eat a variety of fish, but they are also eaten themselves by larger birds and small mammals.

These impala herbivores are in danger of being caught and eaten by the lioness, a carnivore.

MAKE A 'FOOD WEB' GAME

You can have a lot of fun making and playing this 'Food web' game with your friends. You will also learn more about living things and the way in which they depend on each other for food. All the living things in this game live in Africa. To make the game you will need some card, scissors, tracing paper, pencils, crayons and a ruler.

NAME: **SNAKE (3)**
EATS: **SHREW**
EATEN BY: **EAGLE**

NAME: **SHREW (5)**
EATS: **LOCUST**
EATEN BY: **SNAKE/EAGLE**

NAME: **EAGLE (2)**
EATS: **SNAKE/SHREW**
EATEN BY: **—**

Rules

The game can be played by up to six players. There are 36 cards in the pack. All the players should be dealt an equal number of cards. If there are any cards left over leave them out of the game – but check that MAN is not one of these – he MUST be included in the game. The aim of the game is to get rid of your cards as quickly as possible. The winner is the first person to use all of his/her cards.

How to play

All players look at their cards. The person who has MAN starts by placing this card down, face upwards. Players then take turns in a clockwise direction. Each player must, if possible, put down a card showing a living thing which EITHER eats OR is eaten by the living thing on the previous card. If you cannot go you miss a turn. In this game, MAN eats everything, so the second player will always be able to put down a card.

Making the cards

Start by tracing the MAN card. Then look at the diagram below and work out what information to put on the remaining cards. For example, you need to make three WARTHOG cards (shown by the number in brackets). Follow the arrows and you will see that the WARTHOG only eats PLANTS and is eaten by LIONS. Don't forget, in this game, MAN also eats WARTHOGS!

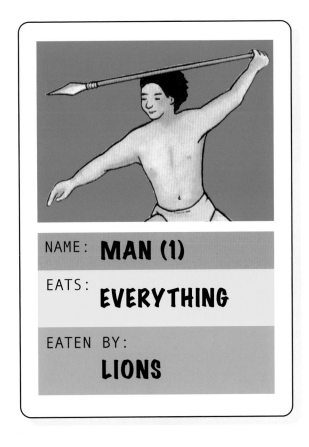

NAME: **MAN (1)**

EATS: **EVERYTHING**

EATEN BY: **LIONS**

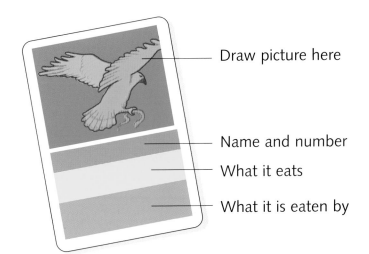

— Draw picture here

— Name and number

— What it eats

— What it is eaten by

ELEPHANT (3)

SNAKE (3)

SHREW (5)

EAGLE (2)

LION (3)

WARTHOG (3)

PLANTS (9)

LOCUST (3)

ZEBRA (4)

MORE ABOUT REPRODUCTION

Genes and chromosomes

Inside the nucleus of a human cell are 23 pairs of chromosomes. Along these chromosomes are 'genes'. Genes control everything about you, including the way you look. Each of your cells has the same genes. You inherit two copies of every gene – one from your mother and one from your father. That is why you look like your parents.

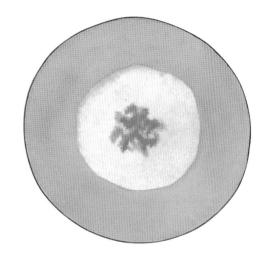

Inheriting eye colour

The gene for brown eyes is known as a 'dominant' gene – you only need to inherit one brown eye colour gene for your eyes to be brown. The gene for blue eyes is weaker. In general, a child will only have blue eyes if both inherited eye colour genes are blue. This man carries a gene for brown eyes and a gene for blue eyes, while the woman carries only a gene for blue eyes. One of their daughters has blue eyes because she has inherited two blue eye colour genes. The other daughter has brown eyes because she has inherited at least one brown eye colour gene.

GLOSSARY

Camouflage
A coloured or patterned appearance that disguises an animal within its surroundings.

Carbon dioxide
A colourless gas found in the air. Plants use it to make sugars and starches.

Cell
A very small part of living matter. Different kinds of cells do different jobs in the body of a plant or animal.

Dominant gene
A gene carrying information that is always expressed in a living thing, even if only one of its type is present in a cell.

Evaporate
To change a liquid into a gas. A liquid needs energy to evaporate and so absorbs heat from its surroundings.

Evolution
The way in which plants and animals have changed gradually over millions of years from simple to more complex forms.

Faeces
The solid waste matter, derived from digested food and expelled from the body of some animals.

Hibernation
The winter sleep when an animal's temperature lowers and heartbeat slows.

Invertebrate
An animal that does not have a backbone.

Mammals
Animals that produce milk to feed their young.

Minerals
Substances in soil water (for plants) or in food (for animals) which are needed for growth.

Nutrient
A substance which provides nourishment, such as minerals.

Oxygen
A colourless gas which makes up about a fifth of the air. Oxygen is essential to the lives of plants and animals.

Photosynthesis
The process by which plants produce oxygen and make sugars and starches from carbon dioxide and water, using energy from sunlight.

Pollination
The transfer of pollen grains from the male to the female parts of a flowering plant, for reproduction.

Sex cell
A cell which has to join with another cell before it will develop into a new plant or animal.

Skeleton
The hard parts of an animal which support its body. A skeleton may be on the outside of the body (such as the shell of a crab) or on the inside (such as the bones of a human or a cat).

Species
A group of plants or animals which are like each other and which can reproduce together. For example, all dogs belong to the same species.

Urine
The watery liquid which carries waste substances out of the bodies of some animals.

Vertebrate
Any animal that has a skeleton of bone or cartilage, with a backbone.

Zygote
A cell formed in plants and animals by the joining together of a male and female sex cell. In the right conditions, a zygote will develop and grow into a new plant or animal.

INDEX

Photocredits Abbreviations: l-left, r-right, b-bottom, t-top, c-centre, m-middle. All pictures supplied by Digital Stock except for: 1 — Corbis Royalty Free. 4tl, 6tl, 8tl, 10tl, 12tl, 14tl, 14tr, 16tl, 18tl, 18ml, 18bl, 20tl, 22tl, 24tl, 26tl, 28tl, 30t, 31t, 32t — Stockbyte. 4b, 8mr, 25tl, 25b — Corbis. 6tr, 10tr, 21, 23b — Photodisc. 6b, 7, 17b, 25tr, 28tr — Corel. 11 — Jack Dykinga/USDA. 12tr — Comstock. 13b — Picturepoint. 15tr — Bruce Fritz/USDA. 22tr — Keith Weller/USDA. 23t — Scott Bauer/USDA. 30b — Digital Vision.